D1340809

WAR

Please renew/return this item by the last date shown. Please call the number below:

Renewals and enquiries: 0300 123 4049

Textphone for hearing or speech impaired users: 0300 123 4041

www.hertsdirect.org/librarycatalogue

Hertfordshire

H46 070 032 4

For Pete's Sake

Katherine Raphael

LONGTAIL

Distributed by Gardners Books, 1 Whittle Drive, Eastbourne, East
Sussex, BN23 6QH
Tel: +44(0)1323 521555 | Fax: +44(0)1323 521666

British Library Cataloguing in Publication Data
A catalogue record for this book is available from the British
Library.

ISBN 978-0-9564528-0-1

Typeset by Amolibros, Milverton, Somerset
www.amolibros.com
This book production has been managed by Amolibros
Printed and bound by T J International Ltd, Padstow, Cornwall, UK

Foreword by
Katherine Raphael

I am a traditional daughter, sister, wife, mother and grandmother who watched with admiration the effort and sacrifices my parents made for my brother. I am a qualified psychiatric nurse and see on a daily basis how families are battered by the emotions of dealing with traumatic situations. I wrote this as a thank you to my parents on behalf of my brother and I would hope that it would help others realise that all their efforts are not in vain and give them the strength to carry on with the knowledge all they do does not go unnoticed.

Although when I wrote this I did not mention the island where my brother and I grew up, I feel now that it is important to say Bermuda was our home and is to where Peter has returned. Thank you for choosing this book. A donation from this sale will go to the

British head injury charity, HEADWAY. We believe this is what Peter would have wished.

List of Illustrations

11   Christmas spent with the family.

12-13 Here I'm on holiday at home with my dad.
     My parents had organised staff to help care for
     me.

14   This is the only picture of me as Peter the Third.
     It was New Year's Eve and I was in a wheelchair,
     my head had to be held up with a strap. I was at
     peace fourteen days later.

Chapter One

There is no single word that can describe a parent's love for their child; what lengths they will go to for their cherished offspring. As I lie here, I witness this extraordinary phenomenon without them being aware, and I have time to reflect on all the reasons for this.

It was 1964 when I arrived on this earth. It was a quiet entrance. I have never been a noisy person and I would always ponder on decisions. Having said that, I did not always make the correct choices, but who does as they negotiate their way along that journey called life?

I certainly had a rose-tinted beginning, adored by my mother and father and fussed over by an older sister who thought I was hers to play with at will. Lavished with adoration, I was growing up a contented little lad. The subtropical island my English parents had had the foresight to move to was one of the most heavenly playgrounds on this earth. My younger days were spent at the beach learning to crawl with the crabs and swim with the fish, which at that time seemed to have no fear of me. Life was just one great big holiday.

I, like everything else in this world, grew older, not wiser. My parents had realised by the time I was seven that they would settle on our island. Islanders are always very possessive; they bought a house and our comfortable world continued.

I went to the only private boys' school on the island. The education was excellent and I started to play the flute. I was really quite good and many Christmases my sister and I would entertain parents with a duet, me on the flute reading the notes and my sister on a small organ reading the corresponding numbers. Her love was tennis. I joined the cubs and progressed to the scouts and at home my interests lay in cooking. I enjoyed my food and was a bit of a tubby lad. Sadly I cannot partake of that pleasure now as my nourishment is pumped into my stomach via a tube, but I can still remember the taste of my favourite spaghetti bolognaise. Birthdays were always spent at our family's favourite Italian restaurant and I could eat more than the others put together.

Another of my favourite pastimes was the traditional Sunday lunch. After church on a Sunday we would often go to one of the hotels and indulge in a buffet the size of an ocean liner. I was always teased at being charged half price but eating a full adult portion. My sister made up for me and had the half-size one. We would then go and swim in the pool or go down to the beach.

There are very few places with beaches made of the finest white-with-a-hint-of-pink sand. You could walk barefoot along the long shimmering stretches, looking out over the sea that would change colours from a clear white to every green and blue imaginable. Some colours probably cannot even be named they are so unique, and you would think you were in Heaven itself. I say this now, but at the time of my youth I was more interested in the games I could play. As a youngster I was content to sit at the water's edge filling buckets with wet sand and building castles that, as the tide slowly come in, would make them melt away.

My own boat, what joy! Now this great joy was only ten feet long and four feet wide and had a racing engine that did not exceed ten knots, but to a ten-year-old boy it was the greatest gift. My best mate and I would spend every free minute we could launching ourselves off into the sound, an enclosed area of water, and after racing the stingray or just racing after our freedom we would settle down to some fishing. Most times we would land on a deserted tiny island, tie the boat up, chuck the anchor overboard and then settle down to our picnic before attaching smelly bait to our lines.

As I look about me, I can see that my family have tried to recreate this divine world for me. If I could I would smile. There are some of the colours of my childhood and the fish are an amusing touch: of course they are nothing like the real thing but you have to love the family for trying.

~ ~ ~

All good things must come to an end, or at least change a bit. My world was about to change and there were other plans for me. It was decided that I would get a better education if I went to boarding school in England. As my parents are as English as you can get, they wanted nothing but the best for their son. Don't get me wrong. They were very happy with the education I had received so far but they felt that I would have so much more, and in truth they were right. My island, although perfect, was like an oasis; the rest of the world at that time did not exist or even matter, and the opportunities awaiting were eye-opening. To this day I still do not know how my sister, who had gone through this a couple of years earlier had managed to prevent my parents from sending her. Admittedly she was more stubborn than I and when she refused to go they must have realized it was not right for her. I on the other hand always went with the flow and so at eleven years I set out on the next challenge of life and flew to England to start school.

As a child my school holidays were interrupted by family holidays. My parents would bring us to England to visit relatives and then visit everything from the Tower of London to castles in Scotland. That reminds me of the time I went for a climb, only to discover that on the other side of the interesting wall was a drop hundreds of feet down into the English Channel. That had the parents' hearts missing a few beats. Anyway I digress - mind you I have the time to - and we could also be found popping across to the continent in a caravan. These holidays were always in the summer. They were enjoyable, except, as I have said, I liked my food, so I was the one who always had wasps after me, apparently because I usually had something sticky attached to me.

School in England was a different situation. Being the laid-back person that I am, I settled in well. There was a fellow islander with me and between us we showed these English kids a thing or two. After my first term we went home for Christmas. When you get off the plane night or day there is a special smell that hits you. I guess it is a cross between salt water and sun, but there is nothing like it, it fills your lungs and seeps through your whole body and you know you are home. My poor sister had the fright of her life when her darling little brother did not seem to walk out of customs, and then this long-haired creature dragged himself up to her and uttered something in a foreign language. She panicked and retreated behind our parents. A lot had changed in a couple of months.

I know now that my parents have regrets about sending me away at such a young and tender age. They were right that it was not for my sister but it was for me. I had a great time, the best of both worlds. I did get an excellent education but I also made some lifelong – that's a moveable feast – friends and we had the best of times and got up to all sorts of harmless mischief. I think I had better stop there, but I do have a smile in my heart.

Five years raced by, and I found I was quite good at maths and science; if only I could use it now. I did well in my GCSEs, so what was the plan now? I'm tired; someone has his or her hands on me.

This twilight zone I am in can be confusing at times, days turn into weeks, time has no meaning, there are what I assume to be routines that are followed at certain times, and as I have no choice I receive them with little resistance. My body does very little and what it does do is only a reflex reaction to what they are doing to me. There is no feeling to anything, so here I am, my body for the outside world to do with as they wish, no pain, so I can carry on with my thoughts.

It was agreed that I could go on to university in America, as my island home was nearby. It seemed sensible to have had an education from both sides of the Atlantic. What a well-rounded person I would become. I stayed at home and went to my old school there. They had a sixth form that would fill in the gaps that I needed to fill to be eligible for America. Back at home took some settling in but it was wonderful and I had a very happy year. I was sixteen and old enough to have a motor bike. It was only fifty cc but by the time my boys (friends) and I had fixed it up it went faster and looked great. My parents never really understood how a brand new bike could end up in so many pieces on the garage floor when there was nothing wrong with it. Part of my coming of age was the redoing of my bike. It had to sound right and look right. Having my own transport gave me the freedom I had never had before; with that I had responsibility for my safety, we took risks, racing our bikes on narrow roads and having the odd beer too many sometimes. We, like most islanders dabbled with soft drugs; there was nothing more than a little herb. Of course my parents worried and there were rows but I was not going to try anything harder and it was just for light relief and a laugh.

My year went all too quickly and I was enrolled at university on the east coast to do computer engineering. Life was sweet and I had a blast. I knew that my first year was going to be a bit wasted, but I was having the time of my life and there was plenty of time to catch up, so I thought. My parents were worried about my commitment but they had faith that I would settle down soon. Their minds were taken up by the marriage of my sister who had gone to England to further her training and fallen in love. I managed to call her once while I was in the US. It was the middle of the night and she was rather pregnant; she was not amused then, but laughs about it now. I was high on the fact that I was to be an uncle.

After a great year I headed back home; the holidays are long and I got a job on a construction site. At least I was showing my parents that I could knuckle down and work. Hot days spent outside and then a night out with my mates was all that a seventeen-year-old needed, plus the money was good.

At the beginning of July my sister, her husband and my three-month-old niece came out for a holiday. It was the first time my parents and I saw our new addition to the family and she was to be christened at our family church. They would also be there for my eighteenth birthday. We kept with family tradition and went to the Italian restaurant; it was still going strong probably solely due to our patronage over the years. After the meal my parents politely retired home and my sister and her husband took a girlfriend and me to a nightclub. I had come of age and my brother-in-law enjoyed the evening as much as I did. I liked girls and they seemed to like me, but I am shy and not openly demonstrative, more a one-on-one type of guy. My sister drove home and we dropped my friend off. They encouraged me to walk her to the front door and take as long as I liked.

They returned to England three weeks later and I was trying to figure out how I was going to explain to this girlfriend the arrival of my old girlfriend from the UK. Confrontation was not my style. I was very fond of this girl in the UK and had said how great it would be if she came out to visit. My life had changed, and it had been a year ago. Still, I liked her, so I thought it would be fun taking her around for a couple of weeks. She did not have the holiday of a lifetime that I had promised her.

Chapter Two

It was the summer of 1982, the heat and humidity had reached a high and as is usual a storm broke out. It always happens and is quite a relief as it cools the place down afterwards. The rain was torrential and inches would fall in a couple of hours. I did not mind, as I knew the weather would soon be glorious and my English girlfriend was arriving the next day. There was only one small problem. We had acquired a small speedboat that had given us years of enjoyment, water skiing, cruising and fishing. We could not remember if we had pulled the automatic bailer plug and, if we had not, tomorrow would find our expensive toy at the bottom of the bay it was docked in. As usual my bike was in bits ready for a new shiny bit of chrome so I used my Dad's bike to pop down to the dock. I was used to driving in these conditions. Unpleasant as it was, it was something you had to get used to on a sub-tropical island. That short trip would change the course of my family's life and mine forever.

The speed limit is twenty miles an hour and I had just left the dock and was driving up the steep hill when it happened. I have no memory of the accident, only the knowledge of what happened from my family and the police. A bus hit me, and it did not stop until I was several feet behind it. As my parents sat reading the Sunday papers they heard in the distance the faint sirens of the ambulance. In this day and age we all hear it so often that only a brief 'poor soul' flashes through one's mind. This time it was their son lying on the sodden tarmac, his body distorted, his face splattered and his brain exposed to the wild elements.

I think the ambulance crew did not hold out much hope, they really did not know where to begin, brain, head, neck all a mess, both legs shattered; but somehow the wheels had missed my torso so the lungs and heart were still going strong.

At the hospital they cleaned me up and patched me up and put me in intensive care. I will never be able to understand the depth of the devastation that my parents felt when they entered the room on that rainy afternoon. All I do know is that they never gave up hope and were to remain by my side forever.

I was in a coma: there's a surprise! My forehead had been smashed and my skull shattered, there was no bone left on the front to protect my brain. Having said that, my brain had swollen so much from the impact that it needed the gaping hole for space. I was not a pretty sight, more like an alien from a badly made old science fiction movie. Amazingly enough, I was breathing on my own and my heart was pumping away almost unaware of the damaged body that encased it. My sister flew back: she did not know if I would be dead or alive. My parents would not leave my side and my poor girlfriend from England was on her way.

There were two of us on the intensive care ward, another young man who had also been in a road traffic accident. He lay there, like myself: there was not a sound to be heard except for the swishing and beeping of various machines attached to us. Two families whom they had never met but both thrown together in a world of torment. Two members of the family were allowed at the bedside only. My sister walked in and there I was, the brilliant sunshine on that perfect day throwing a golden mist over my body. I was eighteen years old, fit and very suntanned, at a glance you could be forgiven for thinking it was some twisted joke; but then you looked at my head and saw the thin flap of skin covering a pulsating brain.

All my parents prayed for was that I would live. When these tragedies happen all you ask for is life: 'Please don't let him die!' How can anyone be rational and think, 'Now let's see, what sort of life will he have, will he ever be able to walk, talk or function in any way?' Parents are the last people to ask.

The first few weeks were just a waiting game. Nobody knew whether I would survive or not. Coma covers quite a range of levels. The family wanted to know when I would wake up, if I could wake, and really the doctors were not sure. A waiting game began. As my niece was three months old, one member of the family would take her out to the gardens while the other two would sit round my bed talking softly or just stroking my hand trying to let me know they were there. Then they would swap and start all over again. My English girlfriend arrived and was picked up by family friends. She was not allowed in intensive care but was helpful and kind to my parents and I will always be grateful for that.

There would be moments of hope and hours of agony as my condition swayed from stable to delicate. There was the deep distress on the morning when I was the only one to be found on the ward: the other young man had died during the night. Who knows why I was still holding on? I was stubborn and there were a lot of people out there praying for me.

After about six weeks my parents were informed that I had come out of my coma. This was a bit hard to take in, as I looked exactly the same. There was not some grand awakening; we have all seen those movies before. They felt that since I reacted to pain I had gained a level of consciousness and they could now declare me ready to move on. The big question was to where. I had a severe head injury; my island paradise did not have the facilities to treat me. They patched up the broken bones and cared for me but now I needed specialist treatment.

If you knew my mother you would understand when I say that if there was anywhere in the world that could put me back together then she would find it. Mind you, she could go off at the deep end now and again and needed my dad to help her take the sensible path sometimes. They were a good team. It was decided that I would be flown to the UK. There was a hospital with an excellent neurological department, and as I was missing most of my frontal lobe, that seemed a good place to start. As was to be the course there was a slight hitch. X-rays showed that I had actually broken my neck. For the three months I lay in the Island hospital I could have been paralysed at any moment, as I was being bed bathed or being given physiotherapy. You had to say luck was on my side.

Chapter Three

When disasters happen, all normal life seems suspended in time. Your world falls apart; all those everyday things seem to get lost in the dark crater you have fallen into. The trouble is nobody else has gone off on a tangent; bills still come in, food needs to be bought and eaten, animals need to be fed, basically life goes on around you and you have to keep up. Insurance is a great thing and I would advise anyone out there to get some. Medical bills add up and there is no possible way for an average family ever to cope with them. It is also not cheap to fly several thousand miles on your back, taking up three seats and being escorted by various medical people. Life had to go on for my dad, he had to keep working and looking after the home that they had both created for their family. Mum had to come with me. My sister and niece had returned to the UK and would be there for my arrival. I know that my father found the pain of us leaving almost unbearable. He wanted to be with me and I know that, but someone also had to deal with the police.

In the UK I was put in a halo; glorious as this may sound it was a confusing and painful time. My neck needed to be stabilised, holes were drilled into my already battered skull and a metal rim was attached and I was stuck there on my back, not allowed to move in case my spinal cord got damaged. I was not able to understand any of this. My swollen brain had gone down but things in there were not functioning properly and I was confused and in discomfort. It was a painful time as I was aggressive towards my sister at times and still did not have the ability to communicate with anyone. My mother was here by herself and my father felt helpless so far away. The anguish that we all had to deal with at that time was more than most families could bear. In the hospital there were many fragmented families who had buckled under the strain of watching a loved one fight so hard for survival.

The winter months crawled by – not that I noticed – and then gradually things began to become clearer. The torture kit on my head was removed and I had an operation to fuse my neck. Operations are not my mother's favourite and each time I had one she would worry herself sick thinking of all the possible catastrophes that could happen. My father was able to fly over to visit, and for the first time it seemed that I could recognise them. The long road to recovery was beginning: there was light at the end of the tunnel. I began to say the odd word, and we could communicate on a very basic level. Then we had another setback. I started to have severe seizures. These are very common in head injuries. You cannot bash your brain around and get off that lightly. We were reassured that in time there were drugs that would control my seizures. They never really mastered that one. There seemed to be another problem. My brain was still under pressure. There was fluid building up and they had to insert a shunt. This meant another operation, a drain had to run from my skull under the skin to my stomach so excess fluid would not damage any more of my precious brain cells. They also felt it was time to rebuild my skull. As the brain went down I was left with a dent that beat. They put a plate under the skin so I would look normal and it would do the job the shattered bone had done before.

After several more months of care and every imaginable therapy, I reached a point where I could walk and talk, very slowly. My patience was not what it should be and I was not inhibited. I was missing the part of the brain that controls that, so I did have an excuse, but if I was to progress I had to relearn a lot. The hospital here had done all they could and it was agreed that we all needed a rest and it was time to go home. My memory was shot and hopefully being in familiar surroundings would set off another learning curve. Travelling was not going to be easy; the numerous drugs I was on had to be administered at the correct time and with the plate in my head, drain to my stomach, fused neck and metal pins in my legs, it was going to be fairly uncomfortable. But I was going home.

It was not going to be the return of the conquering hero. I still needed full-time care and could not be left on my own. I was disorientated and a seizure could strike me down at any time. They were of the grand mal type and I would collapse, fit and then sleep it off. I would have no recollection but each one would cause distress to whoever was with me.

Back home my parents tried to care for me themselves. My father was going out to work each day and my mother was taking on the role of caring for a child that needed constant attention; the trouble was I had the body of a fully grown man. I was happy to be home but could not convey this and I became frustrated. Mentally and physically, I was so compromised that just getting up and dressed could take several hours. I had lost my taste, was partially deaf and my eyesight was flawed; all this made daily tasks mountains to climb. My mother was exhausted at the end of the day and father would help in the evenings. This meant that when he went to work the next day he would be shattered. The time had come for outside help. We had nurses coming in to give my parents a bit of a break. I had some old school friends who would pop in and visit me. I did begin to remember them and we did have some great chats.

I had no control of what I said, things would come out of my mouth and many times I should have kept quiet. My parents discovered a great deal about what their teenager son got up to. I also put them in embarrassing situations. When we went out I would calmly comment on the way someone looked in a loud voice. This was not always favourable and I could have started many a street battle.

I was slowly improving, I was happy; I was having physiotherapy and being cared for by my beloved parents. I could not see the strain it was putting on them, they loved me and that was all I felt I needed. They had other plans. I have said that my mother would go to the ends of the earth to help me. She was looking. A rehabilitation unit was found in America. Physically I was stronger; I had a suntan and was looking good. It was now time to work on my damaged brain. We needed to get it working a little better. The aim was to get me as independent as possible.

Chapter Four

I was taken up to the unit and the next stage of 'rebuild Peter' began. The unit was extremely well organised, and the facilities were second to none. I was assessed and a strict regime was put in place. The nursing staff was caring and happy and my parents felt confident in leaving me there and returning home to sort out the pieces of their shattered lives. I remained blissfully unaware of what they went through.

The fact that a public transport bus had been the instrument of my demise caused several problems. The police had initially charged the driver with driving without due care and attention and had successfully found the driver guilty. The driver was fined and disqualified from driving for a certain amount of time. My parents did not feel that justice had been done. Not only that, but someone had to pay for the treatment and care I would need for the rest of my life. I supposedly had a normal life span in front of me, even with my disabilities. The trouble was the same company employed my mother. They had given her time off to cope with me, many people we felt thought I would come back well and fit. Nobody could grasp the extreme problems that someone has, who is missing an essential part of the brain and trying to use the bit that is left which is also damaged. You had to see it to believe it. My mother had to resign: you can hardly sue your employer, and this was difficult as she had an extremely high-ranking, challenging and enjoyable career. It would take several years, meetings and enough paperwork to save a small tropical forest before a court date and trial would be set up. This cost my parents a great deal. Actually all and more of their money. They had a charitable donation to help them at one stage to keep me in my rehabilitation unit. Nothing was going to stop me from getting the best!

A date had been set; they were relieved and terrified at the same time. They needed to make sure that as they were not getting any younger there would be something in place so that my future care would be catered for. They also knew it would be the first time they heard in graphic detail the moments before, during and after, when their precious flesh and blood son had been smashed, crushed and ripped apart. Both my parents had been good Christians. In my childhood we had gone to church every Sunday. At this time there was quite a bit of ranting and raging as to why this had happened to them, it was not fair; but also they needed to have hope. Faith gives you that.

My parents would come to visit me frequently; I was always delighted to see them. They had several meetings with therapists and doctors, always looking for improvement always asking what more can be done. They did see me slowly making some progress, I could make a cup of tea, I had started to sign my name on cards: these small tasks were the greatest achievements. I was very proud of myself and all along the way with each minute step they praised me to the hilt. With me they smiled. They were positive and we had some very happy times. They then would go home to await the final outcome.

Without boring you with the details, we partially won the case. Nobody really won. I would never be the son they had, the driver would have to live with the sound and sensation of my body under the wheels every day of her life, but my parents would be able to give back the donation, to help another person in need and set up some financial situation for me. My father dealt with this side of things. He had to make sure that I would always have the money to support me. To care for someone like me is a full-time job; not only is it time-consuming but emotionally draining too. As I improved in some ways I still had setbacks; my seizures were getting worse and more frequent, they were life-threatening, and every one I had put my parents through a living hell: again the question arose of would I survive. My father took early retirement; he wanted to devote more time to my future and me.

~ ~ ~

I spent several years in America. I had a 'buddy'. He would come and take me out for trips. I had loved photography and he helped me take some pictures. We did everything from animals to monuments. I would never be able to remember what we had done but the photos always provided me with a sort of memory and at times I think I did really remember. My conversation was limited. I remembered things from my childhood and so I repeated myself often. I still had a dry sense of humour and I made a girlfriend; we enjoyed each other's company and my parents would take us out for a meal on a visit. All this happened under the careful supervision of the staff in America. Once my sister and brother-in-law came to visit and they took me back to my Island for a holiday. Those were happy times. I was able to swim a few strokes in a pool, visit a beach, sit on the veranda and play card and board games with my niece. It was one of the first times my family had been altogether. The only problem I had were these seizures. Again they were getting worse and everything we tried did not seem to help. I was a challenge for the medical world. The other change in me was spiritual. As a young teenager I had believed in survival of the fittest. I had kept myself strong and although I'm ashamed to say it now there was a time when I felt those not perfect were a waste of space. I also went off God. These were mere teenage flexing of muscles, and being the quiet chap that I am I did not make a big fuss and bother, so few people knew this. As my time in America progressed, I realised I was glad just to be here. I praised the dear Lord for all my blessings. I was happy with what I could now do. Being alive and having a family as close as mine was what life should be about. It did not matter that I could not see them every day, my room was filled with pictures, photos and I got tapes from my sister; as usual she chatted on for ages and my brother-in-law had a chat and my niece sang to me. I may have had my limitations but life was good.

I loved my time in America, the rehabilitation unit was warm and friendly and they did an amazing job with me. Doctors who had originally cared for me would never believe that I would have achieved the level of function that I regained. Having said that, there is only so far a brain can be retrained and I had reached what they felt was my full potential. There were very few centres for people with head injuries and it was time for me to move on and give someone else a chance. I returned home to my island once again. My parents pulled out all the stops and every available therapist and carer was put into place. My seizures became worse

1 *My lovely, wonderful boat with me in charge.*

2 *Playing the flute at home at Xmas.*

3 Traditional kite flying on Good Friday.

4 I'm in the middle with my mum and best friend Stephen. We were camping on a small island at home.

5 My eighteenth birthday lunch with my parents. This was taken only a few weeks before the accident.

6 *(Above) My parents on a visit to see me in America when I was in a rehabilitation unit.*

7 *(Left) My birthday with my nieces.*

8 Me with my younger niece at her christening.

9 Me with my sister, enjoying a Mother's Day lunch out with all the family.

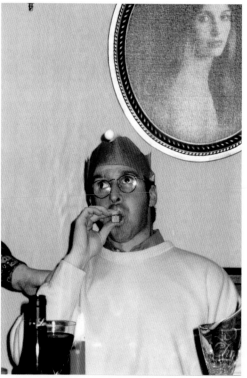

10 (Above) Me with my elder niece on her birthday.

11 (Left) Christmas spent with the family.

12 & 13 Here I'm on holiday at home with my dad. My parents had organised staff to help care for me.

14 This is the only picture of me as Peter the Third. It was New Year's Eve and I was in a wheelchair, my head had to be held up with a strap. I was at peace fourteen days later.

and I still had little inhibition and could still become frustrated and angry. It would lead to several difficult situations. I could easily have a fit any place and time. I would be sitting in the car on my way somewhere nice, and off I would go. Trying to drive a car with someone thrashing about violently is not easy, and when it is your son it is soul-destroying. You think you have planned a treat and it all goes wrong, you think maybe it was the excitement; but what is the alternative, to sit at home and play the same card games hundreds of times because I enjoyed them and never remembered that I had just played them. I could not watch much television as my concentration was poor and I only liked old half-hour comedies that I remembered from my youth.

Even essential jobs became possible explosive situations. I could become angry in a supermarket and hurl verbal abuse at anyone and everyone in spitting distance. People would become cross back and they could not always tell there was something wrong with me, that I just could not help it. My family always had to step in and protect me. I have some sympathy here with anyone suffering from a mental illness. As a society we avoid 'different' looking people and keep ourselves cocooned; it is a sad way for the human race to have gone.

Again my parents wanted more for me and they knew that they could not physically and mentally look after me forever. As it happened there was a unit at a hospital near my sister's home in the UK and this we hoped would help me develop a few more skills to become more independent.

Chapter Five

What a disaster. I arrived in good shape but I hated the place. The other patients were not like me, not that any head injury is the same but this was the wrong situation for me. My family could tell I was upset and my behaviour was unpredictable. All concerned felt that I should at least be given time to settle in and maybe things would improve. They didn't. Something had to be sorted out and soon. Again we came up with the problem of finding somewhere suitable. A new house was being set up locally with full-time staff to care for head injury people in more of a home environment. For people like myself we need to feel secure in our familiar surroundings so it is important that we have possessions that we can easily recognize around us; and it helps to become a little more independent if we know through repeated tasks where we are. I got the best room, a big bay-fronted bedroom facing the front. My family set about decorating it my favourite colour: everything was green. Trunks were unpacked and the bedroom was transformed into my world. Big posters of my island, Bob Marley smiling, and my family all surrounded me in my bedroom. As this was a new venture for the people setting up the unit, there were teething problems. We had to learn to live as a family; cooking for ourselves meant shopping. This was not an easy task; we had a mini bus and would venture out to a supermarket. I would wander round with a member of staff and help choose the food I remembered that I liked. I had lost the taste mechanism, and everything was done in a slow methodical way so I would not get confused. I started to enjoy these trips and this gave me confidence to try more. We went to the pub, I had a pint, and it reminded me of being at school here. I was able to lead a very basic but enjoyable life. Activities were organised for us and we were asked to be involved with the day-to-day tasks of life.

I even took up horse riding for the disabled although with hindsight it was not such a great idea. Don't get me wrong, I loved every minute of it. Falling off and breaking my collarbone was *not* the plan. Having to have an operation did not sit well with my mother who blew a fuse. For me to have a general anaesthetic is not as easy as it is for your average person. The amount of medication I was on for my epilepsy and other things meant it could be a bit tricky. I was fine, but the recovery period was a nightmare. I would forget and suddenly a movement would send me into excruciating pain and then a terrible temper. Needless to say I did not carry on!

My sister lived in the same town and she could pop in and visit any time. It also meant that from then on all high days and holidays were spent with her and her family. As I said my short-term memory was not great. I could be sitting having a cup of tea with her and then she would nip to the toilet and when she came back in I would greet her with enthusiasm and she would have to remind me that she had been there for ages. It was still a joy to see her. I had a new niece, my elder niece was seven and so I could remember her without any problems. Somehow I managed to remember my new niece from day one. Maybe the love for family surpasses everything. My poor parents had travelled a great many miles to be with me in whatever continent I was. The time had come, they decided, to move closer. They felt it was unfair for my sister to take the responsibility of my care, as she had a young family and one day when they were with us no longer it would fall to her anyway. They moved to a village nearby. Now I had what I valued most, my whole family in the same place.

At Christmas we would all go to my sister's and the fun I had was immeasurable. I had nieces who when they were young would play games with me continuously, my father and brother-in-law would sit and have a cigar after a delicious meal that my sister had prepared. I was able to join in with the silly cracker jokes and the opening of gifts for all. I enjoyed shopping for my family. My sister would take me out and I would take ages choosing the right cards. The wording was important to me: it had to truly express my feelings. I was still different and sometimes people would stare but it did not bother me and I seemed to amuse my sister and nieces quite often. There was the time when we were in a shop and the stranger beside me sneezed. I immediately turned to this woman and with hands held in prayer asked the dear Lord to bless her; she made a quick exit and the family were smiling broadly.

During this stable part of my life, I went to Church. I had not thought about it since I was a young lad and events had overridden anything I might have done in my life. I found great comfort in the family of God. I was not judged or stared at. People were patient with me and actually listened, they were not in a rush to escape, they conversed even though I repeated myself often. I enjoyed my time in Church, although in what seemed to me another lifetime I had thought only the fittest deserved to survive. I praised the Dear Lord for getting me to this stage; I only had thanks to give. Others may have looked at me and felt pity; all I had was the overriding joy that I was alive and with my family. Maybe when you have your life almost taken away from you and there is no going back to what you were or wanted to be you are abundantly grateful for every single second you are on this earth. Every day was a celebration for me: each time we went to the shops, every time I saw my parents walk through the front door. As I said I could never remember so they might have seen me the day before and said they would pop in again the next day, but each time it was always such a surprise. In some ways I was luckier than most people, as each day held a delightful new beginning.

Life settled very nicely for me. Unfortunately, my seizures did not improve and I always had to go for the grand ones. I could not be alone for any length of time. I would without warning collapse and have violent spasms Falling, I could hurt myself, from convulsions I could hurt myself, biting my tongue, choking, any life-threatening misadventure could befall me. Sadly, I seemed sometimes to have one fit after another; breathing tended to be a bit difficult at this point and I would need treatment on the spot. Luckily for me, my sister had married a doctor, so when I was with them my brother-in-law could administer the necessary enema or injection, depending on how bad I got. It was too much to ask of my parents so we often had someone with us when we went out. One of my carers became a friend. There was something about him; he was a qualified nurse and the most interesting of people, and he was calm and always seemed in control of a situation. We had a wonderful connection and he would take me out on his own. I had enjoyed a bit of photography in my youth and he showed me again and again how to take pictures. My parents began to have a great deal of confidence in him and one day decided that if I ever was going to make it back to my island home they needed someone like him to accompany us.

I never stopped talking about home, to anyone who would sit long enough for me to describe it, and recount stories of my fishing, camping or any activity that came to mind. To be told I would be going home for a holiday was almost too exciting. Everyone worried about the onset of a seizure. The trip was finally organised and my parents, my friend and I set off. I think they were all totally exhausted by the time we got there. Not me. I could see the sea and all the colours around. The sky with every shade of blue, the houses all painted in their owners' favourite shade and the sea as clear as the palest of crystals. I knew that I could not smell the unforgettable Island musk but I remembered what it was like and I almost felt I really could. This holiday was the most beautiful occasion I had had in many years and it would turn out to be the penultimate time I would come home.

Chapter Six

I had had my accident a couple of weeks after my eighteenth birthday. The years were sliding by and although it meant nothing to me we were all getting older. I was happy in my small world. I did not fully realise how hard my parents worked to make sure that I had the best standard of life possible. There were always meetings going on to try to improve the situation and my parents both expected a high standard of care. They were also always on the look-out for some answer to my seizure problem. I often had to be hospitalised, as I would not stop fitting. The pain these hospital stays put my parents through was excruciating. I would come round after being asleep for a day or so and I would bounce back to myself, quite cheerful really. They felt it was another nail in my coffin, and they took a lot longer to recover. I was, unknown to me, childlike in many ways. I had to have the attention of the person I was with, I could be all-consuming and this is draining for the others. I must reiterate that I was not aware of this and all I knew about was the great time I was having. My parents had to have the occasional time off, and between them and my sister they were able to have a break as long as one or two members of the family were on hand in case of an emergency. I really had no idea how their lives revolved around mine and every decision that was taken always had some reference to me. We managed this situation for several years and we had a balanced life. My two nieces were growing up and I was a part of their lives, an important part. It was good for them to be aware of others that are not as lucky as them and feel comfortable with disabilities. My family included me with their friends, and I was always treated with respect.

I shared my house with two other men with head injuries. The complexities of our new characters are hard to understand. All brains work differently and our behaviours were all diverse. Unless you have had a member of your family changed so dramatically it is impossible to understand. For the people who are left to deal with you, it is like swimming through a sea of jellyfish, and the emotional turmoil of being with us can bring a stinging pain at every stroke. Somehow I want people to understand how our altered lives destroy the lives of so many others. We mainly carry on, as we have not got to worry about anything. Our every need is catered for and we have no comprehension of the toll it takes on the ones we love. Many families break under the pressure. They disagree about what is best for us, they may be fighting a legal battle for compensation; this is only to get what we need for our very existence. Or they just cannot face the reality of the person they once loved having changed beyond recognition. I had the best family and they stuck it out. I do not condemn the families that are not as strong; we must all do the best we can. My family came through, but there was more to come and how would they deal with that?

My parents had stopped their lives to some extent for me. My father had taken early retirement, my mother had left her job and they had uprooted themselves from their life on our Island and moved here to the UK. They had had to start all over again and build a half-life around me. I was not complaining and neither were they. We had established a fairly happy way, with the odd pitfall every now and then. It could have gone on for a very long time; I was only thirty-two years old and healthy, odd as that may seem. I somehow managed to get chicken pox. As a child my mother had been quite happy for me to mix with children, as she felt it better to get these things over with. I refused to get it and it had all but been forgotten. Any adult that gets chicken pox suffers a great deal. I know there are concerns about male fertility, but that really was not an issue for me. My problem was dealing with the discomfort and having self-control not to rip my skin off. The other worry was the fact that high temperatures can bring on a seizure in the fittest of people; for someone like me who could have them at the drop of a hat it was worrying.

~ ~ ~

My sister had taken a part-time job and had popped home to have lunch with her husband. He had been in the area where I lived and had visited me just before they met. He was pleased I did not have too awful a rash but had reminded the staff that I had to keep my temperature down. My sister spoke to my parents, as they had not visited and she wanted them to know that I was ok. The last thing they needed was shingles. Sadly for us all, I started seizing and it went on and on. An ambulance was called, as the medication I was given did not do its usual trick. The ambulance crew tried to stop the seizures, my parents were called and told I was being rushed into the hospital; 'Here we go again,' they must have thought. At some point someone called my brother-in-law. The trip to the hospital is a short one but somewhere on that journey my heart stopped, not the best of things to do. When I arrived at the hospital the attending doctors saw a youngish man with chicken pox who had had a heart attack. They sprang into action. They were going to save me, great! They sadly wouldn't know the suffering their heroic actions would cause. My parents were at the hospital, not allowed near me at that time: understandable. My brother-in-law arrived and went straight to me. I had arrested about twenty minutes or so before and they were still working on me. My brother-in-law was concerned about the effect this would have had on my brain after a period with no oxygen. As it turned out he had good reason to be worried. He wanted to tell them to stop: they had no idea that my brain was not all there and that what was left was also damaged. They got the ticker going again and I was taken up to intensive care.

This was the beginning of Peter the third. Our lives would change again, and this time there would not be any laughter or family days. This was the beginning of a long and painful journey, another test of family strength. How much more could we endure? My parents were taken back to the time they had first seen me after the accident. Nobody could tell them if I would live or die. Moreover, nobody would say what condition I would be in if I survived. Is it really fair for anyone to go through the same life or death scenario with the same child? After all they had done for me, was it fair that I was back to square one or in even worse a condition than before? They must have sat by that bedside in intensive care totally numb. Could they possible struggle on? Do all they had done before? They were older now; did they have the strength? If I could have, I would have told them the answer. I was their son, they had been with me every step of the way, and they were not going to leave me now.

Chapter Seven

To say the family was shell-shocked would be an understatement. My mother was inconsolable. How could this have happened? Was I not being cared for? Often anger is a dangerous substitute for grief, blaming someone else because the pain is too much to bear, and in some crazy way trying to take the misconceived guilt away from oneself. Mother wanted answers then and there. The doctors in intensive care were bombarded with questions they just could not answer, and knowing Mum she could become pretty hysterical. Dad was almost silent; the depth of his pain had no bottom, like parts of the ocean that surrounded my Island. There was nothing anyone could do at that moment. All that could be done was to keep me monitored, stabilise my drugs and wait and see what I would do next.

NOTHING. I was in intensive care for a week or so. After having the most alien-looking of rashes, I managed to start looking normal. As my sister said, I had gone to great lengths to sleep through the most uncomfortable of skin ailments! Especially as she had had it as an adult and had had to use will power and a lot of hot baths not to scratch. I was breathing on my own and so I was moved onto a ward, or to be more precise, I had a side room. I needed total care. The National Health Service has dedicated staff, and although this is not a party political broadcast, they do not have enough staff to go round. My family would take it in turns to sit with me. My favourite tapes were played, I was read to, I was shown photos of all the wonderful times we had captured on film, even my younger niece would come and do her homework in my room. She was tested on her spellings and her reading and she even sewed. All the time I showed no response. Hope was not going to be given up that easily. I had been like this before and there was no grand awakening then. I needed more stimulation and more physiotherapy. I was put through my paces in bed. Then I graduated to being taken down to the physiotherapist's gym. I was placed on a table, strapped in and turned over. Lord knows what it was supposed to help, but nothing happened. There was the odd misguided comment from some people that they were sure I flickered my eyes in response to them but my sister worked long and hard on that theory and I never managed to communicate with her. Tests were being done on me all the time to see if I was in any way aware of my surroundings or if I had any feeling. The most basic instinct is pain. I would not respond to anything. Needles were not a problem. This began to concern those around me: if I did not react to pain what level of awareness was I on?

The house-holders where I had been living were beginning to realise that I was not going back there and they were asking the family to come and take my things away. They had a waiting list and if someone else could benefit they should. To take down the lovingly put together room of my dreams must have been heart-breaking. Life was not perfect but I had been very happy there. It meant accepting the truth. I was not going back.

My mother was on a mission. I had private nurses coming in during the day to make sure that all my basic needs were dealt with, and then they would carry on with tasks to try to stimulate any part of the brain that might have a little spark left in it. It had been several months by this time and the doctor in charge of my care was beginning to realise that I was not showing the slightest bit of improvement. My family was not ready to settle for her bleak diagnosis. Neurologists were brought in and even a crystal therapist came. I'm sure the regular staff on the ward were flabbergasted at the intensity that my parents put into their efforts to bring me back to them. The most astounding thing to me is that my parents were in total despair. Trying to deal with their own grief at losing their son a second time was tearing them apart, and yet to me they were a united front. Mother always dealing with my basic day-to-day needs and Dad helping in that way too, but also dealing with financial and practical issues.

~ ~ ~

My mother the hurricane, my dad the calm eye in the middle. Things were not going well and I developed an infection, which seems to get most people who stay in hospital for a long period of time. The ward wanted my side room, and that did not sit comfortably with my parents, as I needed so much stuff around me. The hospital actually got to the point of wanting me to be discharged to a nursing home. They knew I would not improve and felt it was the best for me, and they needed my bed.

I was in a vegetative state. It was felt that there was no activity above my brain stem. That was keeping me breathing and that was it. Does one get a choice of what vegetable one can become, because I have always hated peas? There is a neurological specialist hospital in London. The consultants there are world renowned. They have been able to help people who have been misdiagnosed and have built up ingenious ways of helping people to communicate, and therefore improve their lives no matter how disabled they have become. That was where I was going. It was not quite as easy as we hoped. I had to be assessed before they would take me, and even then I would have to wait for a space. This unit is the best in probably the world, let alone the country, and the patients need a great deal of care, and progress is slow. I was accepted; I do not think the doctors had much choice. Now I waited. For me this was not a problem as you can imagine; but my family was about to have their first Christmas without me in a long time. Of course they visited me, but I was never going to pull another cracker or play a card game again. Positive thoughts were being sent from friends all over the world and in the New Year I was transferred to London.

The hospital itself was grim. The old buildings were in need of a facelift and the wards were bare. The staff were positive and cheerful. This must have been difficult, as few of the patients could communicate. They also had to deal with distressed family members who always wanted to know what was being done for their loved ones, and had there been the slightest indication of improvement?

Tests were carried out, any activity in the brain above the stem would be encouraging, and it would mean there was something to work with. Yet again my parents decided they had to be near me, so they rented a flat. They would take it in turns to sit with me, play music, read and chat. Always looking for that flicker of recognition, maybe a turn of the head, a squeeze of the finger, a blink of an eye. They were determined to find me somewhere in that body they recognised. My mother insisted I was there, she could not accept I had gone. But had I? There I was lying there breathing on my own, I looked the same, so where was I? Some people have been in comas and woken up saying they felt no pain and they were aware of things going on around them but just could not get the body working. It was as if it was taking a well-needed rest; and when it had recuperated it would let you use it again. Hearing is the first thing to come back and the last thing to go, and you are always told that, so never discuss in front of the patient anything you do not want them to hear. I stayed in London for several months. My consultant was the best but even he had to admit there was nothing he could do for me. There was absolutely no activity above my brain stem and there never would be any change in my condition. All we had to look forward to was the deterioration of my body. At this point my mother decided it was not going to be long before medical science would be able to carry out brain transplants and I had to be cared for until them. I'm not sure what I would have said if I had heard that one but I'm sure I would have expressed some concern about not being me anymore, after I had stopped laughing. Here comes the big question: actually there are several big ones. Where was the bit that made me Peter, different to anyone else in the world? Was it my brain? Was it my soul? What is a soul?

There I lay, looking good I have to say. I was clean-shaven, dressed in a tracksuit and oblivious to it all. My family had my body to care for now, but they would never be able to hear me: I was lost to them. They would have no idea what I wanted, they had to go with their gut instincts; this could cause arguments as they were three different people trying to do their best for me.

Chapter Eight

The life of Peter the third would never change. I had to move to a place of care. One must remember that I'm still only a young man in his early thirties. The last place the family wanted me to go to was a home full of (I apologise now) old people. I still needed stimulation somewhere that would be able to cope with my medical condition, but also treat me with dignity and even a little bit of hope.

On yet another mission, my family checked out the limited places that would accept someone in my condition. Practically they wanted to be as near to their and my sister's homes as possible to make visiting easier. There are very few comfortable places for people like me to go. Some people who do not have the staunch family that I do are sadly left in unsuitable wards. Not me: a lovely home was found. The staff were kind and caring to us as a family unit. The individual rooms were light and had outlooks over a well-maintained garden.

Behind this was a school playing field and beside us a paddock with some friendly horses. Although this was irrelevant to me, it made my family more comfortable.

My room was decorated in the same feverish dedication and the fishes and colours were a pleasant change for the nurses who tended me. Tend me they did!

This part may be difficult for my parents: it is not meant to be. I was to all intents and purposes bed-ridden. My body could not function on its own in any way. I was fed at night through a tube into my stomach, all the nutrients one needed did not do anything for the taste buds. I had a catheter in place; this is a tube inserted inside the penis and allows urine to drain into a bag. My bowels had to be regulated so I did not have the constant problem of lying in faeces, although not uncomfortable for me it would cause sores on my skin, and others would not really want to be near me.

When you do not use your muscles on a day-to-day basis they stop working for you. They contract and become very stiff. Physiotherapy is needed daily to stretch them out. Even with the intense therapy I was having, my arms were determined to cease up. I had splints made, and each morning after my wash and physiotherapy I had these put on my arms to try to stop them contracting more; the skin was breaking down and this could lead to infection, so it was vital to keep the skin dry. My fingers were also contracting and special supports were made for them to stop my nails digging into the flesh: another source of infection. It was a constant battle to stop my body hurting itself.

My wheelchair was adapted so that I had a neck rest and my head had to be strapped to it so it did not flop forward; and as I was constantly dribbling all the moisture would be trapped in the folds of my neck, and again an infection could develop. As you can imagine it would take two staff all morning just to get me up and in my chair. Sometimes I would have an accident and they would need to start all over again. My life had become one long war against the ravages of decay.

On sunny days I could be wheeled out into the garden and almost daily a member of my family would be with me. They would push me around the garden chattering on or sit with me listening to my favourite music that they had heard a million times. The home I was in had activities organised daily and although I could not partake I would be in the lounge with others. I still had various therapies: the hydro pool was one example. I would be put into a type of hammock and lowered into it. This was supposed to be good for my well-being and my skin. How was I to know? I could not feel a thing.

My parents rented a flat nearby so one of them could be close at hand while the other was either at home or having a break from the constant care I needed. I am sorry to say but this is not a life anyone should lead. They had given up their futures to make sure I had a comfortable life no matter how limited. Now they were eighteen years after my accident looking on, wondering what more could be done. My health was deteriorating daily; the sheer physical effort to keep me free from infection was a monumental task. My optic nerve was not being used; I could not register what I was seeing so it began to shrivel like all the other muscles not being used. I do not want to bore you to death with the slow process of the collapse of my body. Sufficient to say that day by day there was less and less of me.

When my parents were with me they were cheerful and chatty but when they left there was despair. My sister would come and be with me and after her usual chatter about my brother-in-law and nieces and their daily lives she would try to ask me what I wanted. I know she felt that this was not for me. In my youth I had been strong and determined and believed in survival of the fittest. After my accident I was more understanding and grateful to the dear Lord for giving me some time with my family. Even with my epilepsy and disabilities, my life as Peter the second had been fulfilling and rewarding. What could I possibly have to say about life as Peter the third? Did anyone get any gratification in watching me now? I certainly did not have the slightest idea whether it was day or night, winter or summer, I did not even know if someone was there or not. My family could have emigrated to the other side of the world and I would not have known. The point is, what was the point in my very existence? I know she worried about my parents. This was destroying them. Sometimes she was so upset she wondered how she could end it all. Would anyone notice if after she left I was not breathing? A pillow over my face would be all that was needed. Honestly would anyone make a fuss and bother? Could she live with the secret of what she had done? My parents needed to be able finally to grieve for me properly. Instead of the pain diminishing with time it was being drawn out. Night and day there were emergency calls. I had fallen out of bed: my catheter was blocked. I was running a temperature. All stations alert, rush me to hospital, insert a needle into my collapsing veins, and pump me with antibiotics: I must be kept whole. The reasons behind this intense care were purely love and devotion for the son they had given everything to. I understand and will never be able to thank them truly. I do not believe that anyone else in the world can have been as loved as I was.

The weeks dragged on into months, a year went by and there was barely a day that went by when I did not have one problem after another. There was a mole on my back. They thought it was skin cancer. I had to have it removed and sent for tests. What if it was cancer, should I go through chemotherapy? Losing my hair would show all my scars from my original head injury, my weakened body would probably never stand up to the treatment and if I did survive how long would it be until some other life-threatening illness befell me? My sister did not want to see me put through any more gruelling hospital cures. How would my parents cope? She was beside herself with worry for them. The pain she saw in their faces was almost too much to bear when she said she felt enough was enough. There was no way she was going to support another long stay in hospital, watching nurses and doctors trying to put drips up and fill my body with chemicals. As it transpired the mole was not malignant.

Chapter Nine

The century was coming to an end. There was great excitement, extraordinary parties around the world were being organised. Resolutions were being made left, right and centre. I had no idea how long this non-state would endure. It had been nearly three years I had been in this condition. The parties were held, no great disaster happened in the world as some experts had predicted, and the life for all continued. I managed to get another chest infection. If you lie down as much as I had to, your lungs cannot work properly and they get infected. I was having difficulty breathing and again I was rushed into the general hospital. The family on alert again dashed to my side. It was the first week of the new millennium. I lay in the bed with an oxygen mask on. The poor doctors had not been able to use any veins in my upper body as they were just plum worn out, so they had a drip in my toe. The pneumonia developed, as all knew it would. My family watched me struggle for every breath, my body convulsing with every hacking cough I could muster to shift the fluid building up on my lungs. The time had come. Although my sister had broached the subject of 'DO NOT RESUSCITATE', before, my parents would not hear of it. This time she was adamant. The three of them sat in a tiny little office, crying and discussing what should happen if my heart could take no more. The very thought of my twisted fragile body being shocked back into action was abhorrent. My parents needed to make the final decision. After eighteen years of fighting to save me with every fibre of their being, it would go against their every belief to say enough was enough. They had to make the right choice for me. They had to let me go. I had not been with them for a few years. It was time to accept my mortality, leave me some dignity, say goodbye and have some peace for us all. All my life they had been making the right choices. They did not let me down when it came to the most important one they would ever have to make. I was still given antibiotics in case by some miracle my body would be able to fight back but it was agreed that if I stopped they would let me sleep.

For several days I was up and down. My mother or father beside my bed day- and if they had not been sent away for some rest, they would have been there – night. It was a cold but sunny morning on January

14th, 2000. I had stopped hacking. There was not a sound, not a twitch, not a tortured grimace on my face. I was at rest. My mother was the first to get to the hospital. She sat with me alone to say goodbye. My father and sister went in together. The hospital staff had washed my face and brushed my hair. I was tucked up as if sleeping peacefully with my arms and hands relaxed for the first time in years by my side. A flower had been placed on my bedcovers. After all we had been through as a family you might expect that we had prepared ourselves for this very occasion. Until you live it you cannot. I hope and pray that my family will have the strength to know it was the right decision. They sat beside me and stroked my hands and brow. There, curtained off from the rest of the ward we were at peace. Grief grips each person in a different way and the sheer practicalities are almost a blessing: they give you a reason to carry on. My family had not finished with their devotion to me. I still had one more journey to make.

Mum, Dad and my sister went to a quiet little restaurant and had lunch. My final resting place had to be discussed. They went together to the registrar's office to register my death. There would not be any complications. My parents went back to their flat and my sister drove to my elder niece's school to tell her in person. My younger niece was being picked up from school by a friend and would be told later. We were and still are a very close family, and I know that I am with them every day of their lives. But it is of fond memories, and they no longer have to turn up at my bedside and try to chat cheerfully along with the knowledge that I could not really hear them, and all they could do was look on at my contorted body.

The funeral parlour collected my body and my parents chose the outfit I would be buried in. Mum, Dad and my sister came to see me. I looked so young. For the first time in three years I was lying straight, my forehead did not have a wrinkle on it and I looked like the young man I could have been. I do not think my family felt the relief that they had hoped for. It was for the best; how could we have carried on? For what did the future hold for me? I would never have been able to touch, feel, smell, hear or acknowledge anyone or anything. I wanted to go home. The funeral was held in the church I had become involved with before the chicken pox disaster. Songs that I loved were chosen and somehow my mother spoke about my courage; although it was not me, it was the courage of two ordinary people leading their lives, planning their future with their family, who had had to change every aspect of their existence on that rainy Sunday afternoon eighteen years before. Their devotion and dedication to me has to be the most courageous, unselfish and unrewarding action that even the most famous of heroes have ever achieved. There are no medals for them, but this I hope will be just a little indication that everything they did was admired and appreciated by me. There were tears in the church, my elder niece wrote and read a beautiful tribute and my younger niece held her grandfather's hand at one point when the pain in his heart was etched on his face. They followed my coffin out with dignity and I was very proud of my family.

I was cremated. A few months later we returned to the most glorious place in the world, and now I am there, a part of my beloved island in the sun. I rest in peace under the clearest of blue skies beside a tree planted in my memory. No matter how far away my family may be, they, one by one, will always return to visit, and now they can sit beside me and smell the air, be caressed by the warm breeze and feel assured that I am happy at last. I love them all and this is my thank you.